From Striving to Thriving

Ra'Lysha Hampson

BookLeaf Publishing

India | USA | UK

Presentation by *BookLeaf Publishing*

Web: www.bookleafpub.com

E-mail: info@bookleafpub.com

ISBN: 978-93-5744-326-5

First edition 2022

DEDICATION

I dedicate this book to my babies Ellisiona and Corleone. You two are the first things I did right in this world. I will do everything I can to build a happy future for us.

ACKNOWLEDGEMENT

-I want to thank everyone who has stood by me through my highs and lows. I wouldn't have made it this far without you.

Depths of Despair

In the depths of my solitude
Reliving the chaos that brought me here
I struggle to find a reason to push forward
As I violently shed more tears
So many unanswered questions
With no purpose insight
How do you know when to give up
When to fight is no longer you're right
Yet I know I have to get back
Back to myself Back to them
My thoughts remain on my loved ones
Even while I am drowning in the deep end
The shadows of my failure
Have such a vast reach
Regretfully I didn't protect you all
Too stubbornly blinded to prevent the breach
Still you must know that I love you
I need you to believe that I care
The uncertainty is eating me up inside
It's damn near too much to bear
Whenever I have hit my lowest
And begin bursting with grief at the seams
I know just where to find you
My darlings I will meet you in my dreams

In My Mind

Here we are again
Left alone with my thoughts
All these unprocessed feelings set in
Forcing me to acknowledge the rot
The decay I speak of
Is fully in my head
The waxing and waning of my Sanity
Engulfs me as I lay in bed
Racing thoughts begin to increase
As I over analyze the days
My past present and future
Whose control I have a little say
But that doesn't stop
My mind from churning away
These what if's can eat you alive
And spit you out with no delay
So I seek help
They say it's the right thing to do
Forcibly overmedicated
Watered down to a state they approve
Why is it I'm at fault
For those who can't handle me at 100 proof
Why must I shoulder the burden
To shrink myself down for you

Am I really that damaged
Full of flaws you can't comprehend
But they must be acknowledged
For my mind to go on the mend
So I save these silent prayers
While fighting unseen battles
In hopes of a future
Where I am no longer shackled

My Light (Ona & CJ)

Painstakingly secluded
In the darkest corners of my mind
I search anxiously for a reason
For these chaotic times I find
Is this a punishment
A consequence of my wrongs
My world ripped away
No piece where it belongs
What have I done
To incur such a wrath
What can I do
To course correct this path
The light once bright
Ignited with optimism
Now shudders with grief
In wait of the next wind
Is this what I deserve
To lose all I hold dear
Was my faith misplaced
In an unsympathetic ear
How can I keep fighting
With this hole in my soul
How can I push forward
With my will about to fold

My babies I have failed you
I have not held up my end
These obstacles cannot stop me
Your hearts I have to mend
Whenever I feel broken
Too defeated to carry on
Your being gives me strength
Infinite fuel to stay strong

Timothy

My dearest husband
Another year we have survived
So much has happened
But we've made it out alive
You lean on me
I lean on you
We must keep each other stable
When peace comes too far and few
My sanity may falter
As it can now and again
But I know you will stick by me
With a helping hand to lend
I know so many people
Have come and gone in your life
Left you broken and hurting
Alone to manage the strife
Please know I am here
To comfort your demons
Help heal the damages attained
Accept and acknowledge your feelings
I have said it repeatedly

You truly have so much potential
To grow and conquer this world
Your combatant spirit will never surrender
So as time goes by
And you blow out those candles
We are in this together
An unstoppable force they cannot handle

Growth

Can I tell you a story
About a woman you may never know
Character forged through tribulations
A lost girl forced to grow
Too much trauma created demons
For protection of her heart
They each took a piece of her
Which ripped her soul apart
So walls were erected
To minimize the pain
Portray what is expected
Instead of the innocence slain
It's time to acknowledge the damages
To heal these raw scars
Can't continue to battle it
Or my peace won't go to far
These demons were my protectors
I give thanks to their relief
But I am in control now
Faith strong in my beliefs

Inmate

Strobe lights flashing
While they begin to recite my rights
I've been here before
There's no reason to fight
Wait to be judged
Wait to be sentenced
Nothing but time now
As they decide my repentance
Are you remorseful
Will you offend again
How stained is your soul
They must weigh your sins
This path I've turned down
Must be course corrected
Or regretfully my life
Won't be the only one affected
I must plead my case
Admit I can be reformed
You see my values and principles
Can never be corruptly conformed
I have a moral compass
Kept constantly in sight
For now I know what's done in Darkness
Will always come to the Light

Sentencing

As time goes by
And that court date draws near
Chaos roams rampant in my mind
Arousing ignorant fear
Fear of the unknown
Fear of what's to come
How do I remain hopeful
With them holding this loaded gun
Admittedly I handed them the bullets
Gave them a reason to pull the trigger
Yet they can't see the whole story
Without it how can my fate be figured
Innocence is a virtue
Left to those young and naïve
I lost it long ago
With idealistic fairytales to achieve
But I swear that it shouldn't be this hard
The trials and tribulations of life
Who should be held accountable
Who should be debted this strife
It is I who must shoulder the burden
I who must take the punishment
But my journey doesn't end here
My redemption will be Heaven sent

My Redeemer By Faith

Living by faith
Is not the easiest walk
I am human I falter
By action and talk
Lord knows I am a sinner
Cannot say I won't sin again
But I know by his word
Through repentance I won't be condemned
You see so many storms
Have passed my way
But I refuse to lay down and die
He walks with me come what May
So whenever my struggles
Become too much to bear
I just plead the blood of Jesus
And I know he will be there

Clarity

All these raw emotions
Flooding through my brain
Clouding my judgment
And amplifying my pain
With no one to confide in
I must bottle it all up
It's bubbling to the surface
Forcing me to erupt
But I must control my actions
I've got to think before I react
Don't let them change your character
Hold fast through every attack
I can't take it personal
For those who lack accountability
Fighting a war within themselves
Forced to endure their own depravities
I know the path I must walk
Our future kept clear in Sight
You are my motivation
For you I will make this right

Hope

Abandon all hope
Ye who enter here
But where there is hope
We have the most to fear
Not knowing what will come
Is a paralyzing anxiety
Trying to stay optimistic
Is to ignore your reality
Yet how can you push forward
Without believing in a better tomorrow
What is your driving force
When your drowning in your sorrow
I try to remain positive
When negativities surrounds
Don't let them see you cry
Or kick you when you're down
You must remain vigilant
When your will is soon to falter
Only you possess the keys
To unlock the tools that alter

To My (Ex) Husband

When it comes to love
Not everything is black and white
Lines become blurred
Unclear on who's wrong or right
This fiery passion shared
Burning deep inside
Unchartered emotions
With no one else to confide
How do we decipher
This tortured romance
How do we decide
Just what to call this dance
Make up to break up
Sealed by a kiss with a fist
What remains is unconditional desire
Though hesitant we take the risk
Each time we build a bond
Then tear it down on cue
On again off again
Understood by very few
Still my heart aches
My body yurns for your touch
How can we let it go
After we invested so much

Our happiness always fleeting
This cycle is taking its toll
My dear you are a part of me
Yet neither soul can control
They say between Love and Hate
There is but a fine line
We use it as a jump rope
Strangled by ties that bind

Acrimony or Matrimony

And so it begins
Your vicious cycle has reset
Dragged along for the ride
So I can pay your debt
All these sweet nothings
Have flown right out the door
Time to brace for impact
While you justify a reason for war
Not sure how long it will last
Your episodes can come as quick as they go
Wondering how I will survive this one
As your family friend or foe
But yet I'm still here
Repeating I signed up for this
I guess I should have known
We never go long without a cruel twist
Never said I was perfect
I surely have demons too
Will they ever play well together
For more than just a fleeting few
Having hope can be delusional
When you're saddled with insanity
At what point do you accept
This brutality as your reality

Which persona should I believe
Dr. Jekyll or Mr. Hyde
Do I stay for the others return
As one eats me alive
I always claim this to be true
To mend my damaged heart
Wait out the darkness
For another loving start
But now I hesitate to get back in line
As the roller coaster begins to board
Too exhausted to pay the toll
Clueless to a fate we push towards

My Fight Isn't Over

Desolate times
Desperate measures
Searching hard to find
A purpose to tether
I've given so much
And lost even more
What's left of me now
Struggles to settle the score
Constantly questioning
Why must I endure
These trials and tribulations
What my future has in store
Once full of possibilities
Now brimming with fear
How can I get it back
What rules must I adhere
I always vowed to never be
Another sad statistic
Focus hard to excel
With each handicap I was fit
I have come too far
To just lay down and die
But I must admit
I'm losing my will to try

With each day that passes
My hope begins to dwindle
Losing sight of my goals
A flame I have to rekindle
As I lay my weary head to rest
Pretending tomorrow will be better
Persistent doubt swarms my mind
A constant pain I cannot severe
What will become of me
If I let agony eat me alive
Will they mourn my failure
Act like I never thrived
I refuse to let them down
No I won't just standby
For you two I will Fight
Sustained happiness will arrive

Friendly Fire

Lost and alone
Abused and battered
Not knowing where to turn
Or if it really matters
Is this all there is
No there has to be more
A higher purpose
To live and die for
Fighting these battles with you
While I'm at war with myself
The damage is taking it's toll
A detriment to my health
Is it possible to recover
To repair what's been done
Can the past be truly forgiven
Can we unload that gun
Yes that ammunition was given
Enough blame to go around
We must take responsibility
Before this becomes Hellbound
Lord knows it won't be easy
The tribulations we must endure
But together we can make it
A solid bond to strive for

Fake Friends

Honesty or Deceit
You decide
How will this affair go
On which side will you ride
If I let you in
Give you the benefit of the doubt
Wait until you show your character
What you are really about
Hand you an inch
See if you take a mile
Try to decipher
What's really behind your smile
You see I'm not the type
To be friendly and fake
So watch how you treat me
Or an enemy you will make

Resolute

Feeling so discouraged
With each win a new loss
Trying to remain hopeful
But my negativities breeds chaos
How am I expected to survive
With one foot held over the edge
Please tell me how I can thrive
While I'm teetering over this ledge
My goals though halted
Remain firmly in View
My determination will never let up
It will always begin anew
Yet my silent scream is blaring
How long will it take
They say he won't give you more than you can
handle
But I swear I'm inching towards a break
It's time to go numb again
To preserve what's left of my sanity
And I vow to stay vigilant
On a quest to unshackle the future me

Severed Ties That Bind

Laying here wide awake
Reminiscing on the Times we had
Memories come into view
The good and the bad
My heart burns for yours
My body craves your touch
My soul needs that feeling
Such an unattainable rush
Then reality sets in
Neither side outweighs the other
And I'm stuck feeling confused
In my relationship with a toxic lover
Lord knows I miss you
I think about you every day
But it's time to accept with regret
We won't be keeping the vows we prayed
My husband I always knew
This was real love that we shared
At what point did we take that turn
Beyond the borders of repair
It's clear to me now
We will never have our happy ending
Our demons don't play well together
I can't spend the rest of my life

Constantly fending and bending
All I can hope for
Is that your truly understand
It kills me inside to realize
Never again will you be my man

Onward Force

Two steps forward
Then one step back
I've fallen again
With only me to pick up the slack
Please forgive me for my sins
My actions I cannot deny
I let my demons roam rampant
Their deprivations are justified
My faults don't define me
They won't decide my future
My babies are depending on me
They don't deserve my failure
My fate is in my own hands
Structured by their control
I must follow the parameters
I must prevent an all time low
Keep my eyes on the prize
To attain true happiness and peace
Can't stop until I get it
My will cannot cease

Your Fight Is Over

I'm not a victim
A silent scream made while tears stream down
my face
As I'm transported to encounters
My mind will not erase
My hair wrapped around your fist
While I'm praying for my life
Or the blood pouring from my head
As I tell my child to hide a knife
How could I love you
Why did I keep going back
I even accepted one day
My demise would come from your unbridled
attack
But I'm not a victim
I don't desire the pity attached to that label
What I crave is my sanity
In a quest to find a fate more stable
You didn't kill me
No I Survived
What's left in your wake
A Warrior's strength I dare not hide

Breaking Ground

The walls to protect my heart
Have become quite lonely inside
I've chosen to let you in
Where the pain and pleasure resides
I'm hesitant yet hopeful
Will you be the one
To withstand all the rain
Steadfast to see the sun
Men have come and gone
Left ruins in their wake
They demolished instead of building
Of what's left of my sacred place
I don't expect you to pick up the pieces
Darling I will rebuild my health
Just hold my hand
Together we stand
As I better my former self

Rebirth

The appeal of a fresh start
Such an unattainable lure
Can the past truly be forgiven
For possibilities of a future to endure
No doubt we all have history
Can't pretend it's all bad
But when judgments are laid to rest
They will only acknowledge the sins you had
Turning over a new leaf
Though strenuous as it may seem
It's only the first impediment
In your pursuit to find reprieve
Try not to get discouraged
Keep your motivations and goals insight
They can implant various handicaps
But they cannot take away your will to fight
So do that you must
For all you hold dear
Your true fate does not lie in
To whom you trust or fear
I was once so captivated
In all I could not control
In reality it's always my retort
That plays a greater role

On progression I will focus
Not what has conspired in the past
I'm no longer that person
This Phoenix will hold fast